HAL•LEONARD
INSTRUMENTAL
PLAY-ALONG

TENOR SAX

PIRATES OF THE CARIBBEAN

HOW TO USE THE CD ACCOMPANIMENT:
A MELODY CUE APPEARS ON THE RIGHT CHANNEL ONLY. IF YOUR
CD PLAYER HAS A BALANCE ADJUSTMENT, YOU CAN ADJUST THE
VOLUME OF THE MELODY BY TURNING DOWN THE RIGHT CHANNEL.

ISBN 13: 078-1-4234-2198-6
ISBN-10: 1-4234-2198-1

Disney characters and artwork © Disney Enterprises, Inc.

WALT DISNEY MUSIC COMPANY

DISTRIBUTED BY

HAL•LEONARD®
CORPORATION

7777 W. BLUEMOUND RD. P.O. BOX 13819 MILWAUKEE, WI 53213

Visit Hal Leonard Online at
www.halleonard.com

◆1 THE BLACK PEARL

TENOR SAX

Music by KLAUS BADELT

small notes optional

p

◆2 BLOOD RITUAL/ MOONLIGHT SERENADE

TENOR SAX

Music by KLAUS BADELT

◆ DAVY JONES PLAYS HIS ORGAN

TENOR SAX

Music by HANS ZIMMER

◆ DAVY JONES

TENOR SAX

Music by HANS ZIMMER

DINNER IS SERVED

TENOR SAX

Music by HANS ZIMMER

◆7 I'VE GOT MY EYE ON YOU

TENOR SAX

Music by HANS ZIMMER

HE'S A PIRATE

TENOR SAX

Music by KLAUS BADELT

JACK SPARROW

TENOR SAX

Music by HANS ZIMMER

◆ 9 THE KRAKEN

TENOR SAX

Music by HANS ZIMMER

THE MEDALLION CALLS

TENOR SAX

Music by KLAUS BADELT

ONE LAST SHOT

TENOR SAX

Music by KLAUS BADELT

⑫ TO THE PIRATE'S CAVE!

TENOR SAX

Music by KLAUS BADELT

TWO HORNPIPES
(Fisher's Hornpipe)

TENOR SAX

By SKIP HENDERSON

⟨15⟩ WHEEL OF FORTUNE

TENOR SAX

Music by HANS ZIMMER

14 UNDERWATER MARCH

TENOR SAX

Music by KLAUS BADELT